YOUR KNOWLEDGE HAS VALUE

C000161169

- We will publish your bachelor's and master's thesis, essays and papers

- Your own eBook and book - sold worldwide in all relevant shops

- Earn money with each sale

Upload your text at www.GRIN.com and publish for free

Daniel Barthold

The Business of European Football

GRIN Verlag

Bibliografische Information der Deutschen Nationalbibliothek:

Die Deutsche Bibliothek verzeichnet diese Publikation in der Deutschen National-
bibliografie; detaillierte bibliografische Daten sind im Internet über http://dnb.d-
nb.de/ abrufbar.

Imprint:

Copyright © 2009 GRIN Verlag GmbH
Druck und Bindung: Books on Demand GmbH, Norderstedt Germany
ISBN: 978-3-640-44002-3

This book at GRIN:

http://www.grin.com/en/e-book/135512/the-business-of-european-football

GRIN - Your knowledge has value

Der GRIN Verlag publiziert seit 1998 wissenschaftliche Arbeiten von Studenten, Hochschullehrern und anderen Akademikern als eBook und gedrucktes Buch. Die Verlagswebsite www.grin.com ist die ideale Plattform zur Veröffentlichung von Hausarbeiten, Abschlussarbeiten, wissenschaftlichen Aufsätzen, Dissertationen und Fachbüchern.

Visit us on the internet:

http://www.grin.com/

http://www.facebook.com/grincom

http://www.twitter.com/grin_com

BOND UNIVERSITY

"The Business of European Football"

Daniel Barthold

Subject: Special Research Project in Sports Management

Word Count: 7200

Course: Master of Sports Management

Index

1   Introduction

European football (soccer) is the most popular sport in the world. The so-called "World Game" was once categorized as the "only one world religion" by FIFA-President Sepp Blatter.[1] In fact, soccer has millions of supporters worldwide and can be named as a sport with an outstanding history and tradition. The Soccer World Cup, for instance, is the biggest single sport event in the world and its huge meaning has an influence even on politics, economies and a huge social significance. For a country like South Africa which will be the host nation of the World Cup in 2010 it can be a historic opportunity to strengthen the economy and the political situation in the country and to curtail the high crime rate. Only a big event like the World Cup is able to release these changes away from social, religious or political divides.

Soccer in Europe is special not only because the sport was established in Europe (England) but also because it is the place of the best domestic leagues and the home of various successful national teams. Due to the various countries on the continent football in Europe has a diversity of culture and tradition which is unique and extra-ordinary. Over the past years the sport has changed intensively. The quality of the game has improved and the sport has become much faster. Furthermore, the best domestic leagues which used to have a very similar level have led into a new era with significant differences. The reason for the change of European football is diverse but the core of the change needs to be found in the business of soccer. The money involved nowadays offers much more opportunities for football clubs and opened a door into a new level of football management and competition. New investors, the penetration of new markets and a higher level of merchandising and sponsorship are only a few examples of the wealth of European clubs. In 2007 the „European football market grew to 13.6 billion Euro which is an increase of 1 billion Euro."[2]

In this paper I will focus on the four most competitive leagues in Europe which are the English Premier League, the Spanish Primera Division, the Italian Serie A and the German Bundesliga. Statistically 17 clubs out of the 20 richest football clubs in Europe are from the

---

[1] Jennings, Andrew (2006). *The Beautiful Bung: Corruption and the World Cup*. London: BBC 1 Documentary

[2] Deloitte & Touche LLP (2008). *Annual Review of Football Finance.* Retrieved on October 17th from http://www.deloitte.com/dtt/article/0,1002,cid%253D56148,00.html

major four leagues (England, Germany, Spain and Italy). Only the two French clubs Lyon and Marseille and the Scottish club Celtic FC are not from those leagues.[3]

Each of the named leagues experienced a unique development over the past years. I will focus on the individual changes in each league, point out positive and negative effects on European football and will finally evaluate the four leagues individually and in the entire European context. The different directions of each league and its outcome are based on a SWOT analysis which identifies the major strengths, weaknesses, opportunities and threats.

Issues like the era of overtakes in England, the benefits of the World Cup for German football, hooliganism and corruption in Italy or the significant meaning of Spanish club football will be analysed in this paper. Moreover, it is necessary to consider the "globalisation of sport" which makes the competition in sports even more intense but also presents new ideas from other sports which can have a positive influence on European football. The analysis includes a future prognosis of football in Europe and its domestic leagues.

2   The English Premier League

English football has experienced significant changes over recent years. Not only the English teams became much more successful in European competitions but the clubs also got a new profile. Compared to other leagues in Europe the Premier League and its major clubs such as Manchester United, Chelsea, Arsenal or Liverpool have become global brands including high possibilities of investment. In business terms the English Premier League is the most competitive football league and adapted well to the changes of sport business. To maximize the number of supporters of the league seen as potential customers the management of the association and the football clubs in England realized the importance of entering new markets and promotion of the Premier League on a global scale as part of the so-called "globalization of sport".[4] Unlike any other domestic football league in Europe the English Premier League faced new competitors from other sports on a high level which can have an influence on the number of customers/supporters of the league. Sports from the United States, for instance, entered the English market in the last

---

[3] Cuddihy, Paul (2008). *Celtic are one of the world's top 20 clubs.* Retrieved on October 17th from http://www.celticfc.net/news/stories/news_140208090337.aspx

[4] Chadwick, Simon Dr. (2008, p. 28). *FC Barcelona: Victory On And Off The Field.* Sport Marketing Europe

two years by hosting league games in London. Either the American football league (NFL) and the North American ice hockey league (NHL) opened its season in London. Purpose for the management of these associations is to enter the English and European market and make more people outside the United States interested in these sports. For the English Premier League it means that the globalization of sport brings new competitors from overseas into the market but it also offers the penetration of new markets to maximize profits. More supporters, wider broadcasting, sponsorship and global merchandising are decisive factors for higher turnovers of the English Premier League and its football clubs. Clubs who realized the globalization of sport now have advantages due to higher profits. One of the clubs which has benefited most from a global strategy is Manchester United. The club is a global brand with the largest number of supporters worldwide and was rated one of the richest football clubs in the world in 2008.[5] In 2007 and 2008 United has not only dominated the English Premier League but the club also won the European Champions League in 2008 against rival Chelsea. The Champions League is the biggest European club tournament. The sporting success of Manchester United shows that the business aspect of each football club is fundamentally important to assure positive financial and sporting outcome. Therefore clubs like United are highly competitive in Europe.

2.1   Strengths – The financial wealth of English club football

In terms of player transfers and investment the English Premier League is ahead of any other football league in Europe. As mentioned the business of football in England is advanced and the four big clubs Manchester United, Chelsea, Arsenal and Liverpool experienced sporting success in Europe. From 2005 to 2008 there have been at least on English team in the final of the Champions League including Liverpool and Manchester United winning the trophy. It is evident that the business strategies of the clubs are successful and offers an advantage towards European teams from Spain, Italy and Germany. The reason for the advantage is first of all based on overtakes by investors. Since 2000 several English clubs have been overtaken which has positive and negative effects on the clubs.

---

[5] Harris, Nick (2008). *Chelsea climb into top five of world's richest.* Retrieved on October 13th from http://www.independent.co.uk/sport/football/news-and-comment/chelsea-climb-into-top-five-of-worlds-richest-781884.html

The most obvious positive aspect is higher possibilities of investment in new players. After Russian investor Roman Abramowitsch bought Chelsea FC, for instance, the club changed completely. Not only the club structure changed but also the team was rebuilt.

Billionaire Abramowitsch made the club able to get one of the best players from England and all around Europe. Most significant effect of the investment was the fact that Chelsea won two English Premiership titles in 2003 and 2004 which were the first titles for the club since 1950. In fact, Roman Abramowitsch invested more than 760 million Euro into Chelsea between 2003 and 2007.[6]

2.2   Weaknesses – England and the investment in human capital

The investment in international and domestic players is one of the most important aspects of football management. Different strategies of clubs have certain consequences on the national team. There is a connection between the sporting success of the major English clubs and the issues of the English national team over the past few years. Usually the clubs and the associations like the Premier League and the English Football Association (FA) work together to invest in young English players to support the national team. Due to the overtakes of foreign investors who only see the profits and are not interested in the success of the national team, the investment changed from supporting the young English football players to the trade of international superstars. This strategy is proven by the issues of the English national team which was not able to qualify for the European football championships in 2008 and the international squad of teams such as Chelsea. Even though Chelsea has two English superstars with Frank Lampard and John Terry, the rest of the team is predominantly international. Players like the Portuguese Deco, the French Nicolas Anelka, German midfielder Michael Ballack, Czech goalkeeper Petr Cech or Didier Drogba from Ivory Coast are only a few examples of international squads in English club football. Therefore, young English players do not have the possibility to play for their clubs which is the reason for the issues of the English national team. Moreover, clubs become more powerful due to their financial strength which causes that the strategy of buying players from other international leagues will not change in the next years.[7] A lot of football associations in Europe are concerned about that development and the world football organization FIFA plans to introduce the so-called "6+5 rule" which requires a

---

[6] Deloitte & Touche LLP (2008). *Annual Review of Football Finance*. Retrieved on October 17th from http://www.deloitte.com/dtt/article/0,1002,cid%253D56148,00.html
[7] Pfahler, Thomas (2000, p 82). *Human Capital and Efficiency* (Published in German language). Paul Haupt Verlag Germany

minimum of six domestic football players in each squad.[8] It means that a club like Chelsea, for instance, would have to have at least six English players in their starting team. This idea would support younger players and their ability to play for the national team.

Compared to England, there are countries in Europe who emphasize on supporting domestic players rather than trading international players. The Netherlands and their strategy is highly focused on supporting Dutch players and having an advanced scouting system. Due to the fact that the Netherlands have a much lower population than England, France or Germany they rely on such a system to be successful on a high level in European football. Especially the two major Dutch clubs Ajax Amsterdam and PSV Eindhoven have brought up a huge number of great players. The scouting system not only focuses on young Dutch players but also on players from South America. Past Brazilian superstars such a Ronaldo or Romario started their career in Holland and Dutch players like Robin van Persie, Dirk Kuyt or Rafael van der Vaart nowadays are examples for good consistent development of players in the Netherlands.

Although a lot of the Dutch players trade to clubs in stronger leagues in England, Germany or Spain, the national team highly benefits from it. After England did not make the Euro Championships the English football clubs and the association realized that young English players need to be supported to assure a long-term success of the national team. Young English players such as Theo Walcott, playing for Arsenal, now play in the first squads to give them experience on a professional level. For the English Football Association the Dutch strategy should be a benchmark to find a balance between English and international players in the Premier League. Therefore, the 6+5 rule can be seen as appropriate for European club football.

2.3   Opportunities - The Premier League and the success in the Asian market

In professional sports nowadays it is impossible to focus just on one market or one single target group. The mentioned globalization of sport requires a business strategy for sporting clubs which focuses on penetrating new interesting markets. The English Premier League is more known overseas than the Spanish, Italian or German football league. In North America European football is recognized but faces the issue of high competition of domestic sports such as American Football, Baseball or Basketball. Most English clubs have realized that the most lucrative market is located in Asia. Not only the large

---

[8] FIFA (2008). *Yes in principle to 6+5 rule.* Retrieved on October 17th from
http://www.fifa.com/aboutfifa/federation/bodies/media/newsid=684707.html

population in China, India or Japan but also the lack of other sports in that area offer clubs huge benefits by entering the Asian market. Most popular club in Asia is once again Manchester United. Statistically 83 million of the 139 million Manchester United supporters worldwide live in Asia which is connected to a gross venue of US$ 478.5 million.[9] The idea of the clubs and the Premier League is to create a relationship to new supporters. The Premier League organization started to host pre-season tournaments in Asia and Manchester United follows a player transfer strategy which not only implements the strength of the squad but also creating a relationship to new potential supporters. The Korean national player Ji-Sung Park, for instance, was traded to Manchester United not only to improve the team but also to create a relationship to the Asian market. It is evident that even player management can have business purposes to some extent. To my mind the Asian market is one important aspect for English football clubs to be one of the richest clubs in Europe. Clubs from mainland Europe face the issue that the English Premier League is more accepted in Asia which makes it easier for clubs like Manchester United or Chelsea to enter this market.

2.4   Threats - Competition within the English Premier League

Sporting success is dependent on different factors. Some clubs have a bigger financial background and therefore greater possibilities to invest in human capital/players. The sporting outcome of a club is highly connected to the financial aspect. Therefore, the investment in human capital and player transfers can be seen as most important for football clubs to be successful.[10] In the English Premier League the competition has changed especially after investors started to buy clubs. Before that time there have been clubs with a stronger financial background and a better squad such as Manchester United or Arsenal London but nowadays the differences within the 20 Premier League are much bigger and the league needs to be distinguished in four different classes. Firstly, the so-called "big four clubs" Manchester United, Chelsea, Arsenal and Liverpool dominated the Premier League over the past years. All of these clubs have high investors behind them. Manchester United, Chelsea and Liverpool have been overtaken and Arsenal is sponsored by the very successful company "Fly Emirates". It is estimated that these clubs are the only ones able to win the Premiership title over next few years and represent the top class of English club

---

[9] CNN (January 11th, 2008). *Man. Utd. Profits shoot up by 93%.* Retrieved on September 26th from http://www.cnn.com/2008/BUSINESS/01/11/manchester.united/index.html
[10] Becker, Gary S. (1994, p 17). *Human Capital.* The University of Chicago Press

football. Next are those teams who generally compete for the qualification for international competitions. Clubs like Aston Villa, Everton Football Club, Portsmouth FC, Tottenham Hotspur or Manchester City have higher amount of supporters and financial background and need to be seen as the second strongest class of the league. Especially Manchester City just experienced financial boost after an investment group from Abu Dhabi bought the club for £ 220 million.[11]

The average teams in the Premier League are clubs with certain financial strengths who are able to reach places for European competitions but are never successful on a consistent level. Clubs such as Newcastle United, Middlesbrough, Bolton Wanderers or West Ham United are known for inconsistency which means that they are able to reach a place for the UEFA-Cup (European competition) but could also be threatened to get relegated. Promoted clubs from League 2 to the Premier League or teams who were close to relegation for several seasons build the weakest block in the Premier League. In the season 2008/2009 clubs like Hull City, Stoke City, Fulham or West Bromwich Albion are seen as the weakest teams. It shows that there is a wide range of different competitions within the Premier League and the differences between the clubs are larger than in other European football. Compared to other sports, football and its associations do not limit the amount of money for player transfers. Major American sports such as the National Hockey League (NHL) or the Australian Football League (AFL) in Australia tries to even the competition by having the salary cap and draft system. That means that teams, no matter how different the financial background, are only allowed to spend a fixed amount of money for player transfers. Furthermore, the draft system allows weaker and least successful teams of a season to pick young players in advance. A positive aspect of this system is that a new season gives more teams the chance to keep up which strengthens the competition within the sport and the league. In European football this system is not common and causes that only the richest teams are able to win domestic and international titles. Although the mentioned different competitions within the league need to be seen different from other sports, the fact that there is no salary cap makes each season foreseeable to some extent. For instance, it can be expected that only the big four teams in England will be able to win the domestic Premiership.

---

[11] Draper, Rob (2008). *Manchester City's billionaire wanted to buy into Arsenal.* Retrieved on October 17th from http://www.dailymail.co.uk/sport/football/article-1053144/Manchester-Citys-billionaire-owner-wanted-buy-Arsenal.html

The development is a concern for the Premier League and due to the grown investment in football players and the high amount of salaries paid, quite a high number of managers involved in the business of football prefer the introduction of a salary cap and the draft system to level the competition and in some way to protect clubs.

2.4.1 The loss of traditional values in English club football

Manchester United is a club overtaken by American investor Malcolm Glazer. Similar to Chelsea, Manchester United has already been a wealthy football club in the past, even though the investment possibilities nowadays reached another step. It is required that the investors are familiar with the fact that tradition has a very high meaning in European football and needs to be considered in the business of football. This fact leads to one of the negative aspect of overtakes: Most of the clubs are losing their tradition.[12] Supporters of the clubs highly criticize the involvement of investors due to the fact that they are selling the tradition of the club and only focus on turnovers. Local supporters in the Manchester area, for example, complain about the strategies of Malcolm Glazer who is more focusing on new target groups overseas and a supporters group of a richer social background. So-called "die-hard supporters" more come from a working class background and are not able to afford tickets for the games in the new stadiums. Therefore the investors did not only rise ticket prices to cover costs for the modification of the stadiums but also to change the domestic target group in England from the lower and middle class more to the upper class. This strategy is the main reason for the negative view of supporters towards these investors. Fans in England see themselves excluded from the Premier League and realized that investors transformed their football club into a global brand for profit purposes.[13] In terms of business it needs to be seen as reasonable to reach new target groups even though the rich football clubs have to realize that the domestic target group in Britain are much more loyal than other target groups overseas. Beside the fact that clubs are losing their tradition which is more a European concern (in the United States sporting success is above traditional values), clubs have lost their most loyal supporters due to the new business of football.

---

[12] Shackleton, J.R. (2000, p. 88). *Football as a business*. London: Westminster Business School
[13] Desbordes, Michael (2007, p. 306). *Marketing & Football – An International Perspective*. Oxford: Butterworth-Heinemann

3. The Italian Serie A

Whereas English club football has been a success story over the past years the Italian football league (Serie A) is the league with the biggest problems nowadays. There have been several incidents before the World Cup 2006 which included huge reputational damage for the Italian clubs and the Italian football association. To analyze the issues and to point out positive aspects of Italian football a SWOT analysis of the Serie A reflects the most important factors of the league. Interestingly the Italian clubs and the national team have always been very successful even in the worst years from 2005 to 2007.

3.1 Strengths – Competitiveness of Italian clubs

The Italian Serie A has a large number of very successful clubs which are highly competitive on a European scale. Clubs like AC Milan, Inter Milan, Juventus Torino, AC Florence or AS Roma are one of the top class clubs in Europe. These clubs are also able to invest in international players and especially the two teams from Milano, AC and Inter, are successful in the Champions League. Moreover, the Italian national team has always been highly competitive as well. There is a large number of very good Italian players in each generation. For instance, there were huge issues in Italian football before the World Cup 2006 which I will point out later but the national team was able to become World Champions.

The fact that Italian soccer faced unique issues but is still having sporting success shows that football in Italy is very strong and competitive.

3.2 Weaknesses – Corruption and hooliganism

From the 1990´s to present time the Italian Serie A has changed from the best soccer league worldwide to an instable and highly critical domestic league. The English Premier League, the German Bundesliga and even the French Ligue 1 and the Dutch Eredivisie shaped up over the past years which make the issues in Italy very concerning. The Serie A faced two issues which are most likely the most dangerous problems for a sports league and its clubs: Corruption and hooliganism. In 2005 several Italian soccer clubs were involved in bribes of referees including big clubs such as Juventus Torino, the most successful Italian football club, AC Milan and AC Florence. Juventus Torino was the club most involved in the bribes and was banned from the Serie A by the Italian Football Federation. As being the most popular club in Italy, Torino lost a huge number of supporters and started the season 2006/2007 in the second Italian league (Serie B). The interest in Italian football declined rapidly and the media and supporters lost their trust in the football clubs and the referees as part of the Italian Football Federation. The corruption scandal not only caused financial losses of the clubs and the departure of several first-class players to other European clubs but also the rise of hooliganism in Italy. Loyal supporters were no longer interested in attending league games and hooligans saw in football stadiums a place to express their violent behaviour. Clubs like AS Roma or Lazio have been known for having violent fans but also other clubs especially from Sicily such as Catania Calcio or US Palermo got a rising number of violent supporters. The causes of hooliganism in Italy are disastrous. The average attendance in the Serie A are dissatisfactory and therefore, the profits of ticketing and merchandising are much lower than in England or Germany (the opposite development in the German Bundesliga will be explained later in this paper). Moreover, no Italian football club plans to modify its stadium due to the violence which results in obsolescence of Italian stadiums. This is another reason why football fans avoid attending Serie A matches and why the application of the Italian Football Federation to host the Euro Championships in 2012 was unsuccessful.

The issues mentioned are evident that the Italian Serie A is leading towards an opposite direction compared to football in England, Germany or Spain. Statistically there was a "236 million Euro reduction in revenues in the Italian Serie A in the season 2006/2007."[14]

3.3 Opportunities – Quality of Italian football and new campaigns

To my mind there are two opportunities for the Italian Serie A to be competitive in Europe. Firstly, international football players from South America and parts of Europe still have a positive attitude towards the big Italian clubs. Just recently one of the best football players in the world, the Brazilian Ronaldinho, traded from Spanish club Barcelona to AC Milan. It not only shows that there is still an interest in the Serie A but also the international sporting success of Italian clubs can be assured by trading top class players. To protect the reputation the Italian Football Federation has the task to put down hooliganism. This is the second opportunity for the Serie A. If the problem of hooliganism will be solved, the reputation of Italian football would be put up and more players would make the move to clubs like Juventus, AC Milan, Inter Milan or even average teams. The clubs in Italy,

---

[14] Deloitte & Touche LLP (2008). *Annual Review of Football Finance.* Retrieved on October 17th from http://www.deloitte.com/dtt/article/0,1002,cid%253D56148,00.html

especially Lazio Roam, Catania Calcio or US Palermo, and its management do too little to solve the issue of hooliganism. Clubs from Britain or Germany actively expressed their attitude against racism and violence in sport and highly benefit from it. The Scottish Premier League clubs Celtic and Rangers were historically known for having violent supporters due to their incredible rivalry. Public relations campaigns by both clubs had the effect that violence has mainly been banned from the stadiums and international players traded to both clubs. Rangers FC, for instance, introduced the campaign "Pride Over Prejudice" to ban racism and violence. Celtic FC traded several international players such as Jan Vennegoor of Hesselink from the Netherlands, the German Andreas Hinkel or Australian Scott McDonald. I am firmly convinced that the reputation of Italian football clubs would improve with similar campaigns by the Italian Football Federation and the Serie A clubs.

3.4 Threats – Competition between the major European leagues

The major threat for the Serie A is the competition in Europe. As mentioned most leagues improved their financial abilities and sporting success and any campaigns or new strategies of Italian clubs will take time and other leagues in Europe will benefit from the issues in Italy. National players such as Luca Toni, Fabio Cannavaro or Fabio Grosso who won the World Cup in 2006 left Italy to play football in Germany, Spain or France. It is a threat that on a long-term perspective the Italian Serie A will be the least profitable league of the top four leagues in Europe. The fact that there is less money involved than in England, the attendance is lower than in Germany and the issue of hooliganism can result in more Italian players trading to other European clubs and less sporting success of Italian teams in European competitions.

3.5 The failure of the Italian club management

The SWOT analysis revealed the major issues of Italian football and possible solutions.

To my mind it is difficult to strengthen the damaged reputation of the Serie A on a short-term basis. It will take time before the league and its clubs completely recovered and more supporters attend the league matches. Even though, I think the management of the clubs, especially those with a high background of violent supporters, need to realize that they have to actively fight racism and violence. So far the Italian clubs have not started any campaigns for reputational purposes which is a major failure of the club managers and responsible persons. Clubs in England or Germany are years ahead in terms of fan relations. This failure will be disadvantageous for the profitability of the league in the nearest future. On the other hand I would like to underline that from a sporting perspective Italian football is still quite impressive. The World Cup victory in 2006 and the performance of AC Milan in the Champions League over the past years are evident that the performance of the Italian national team and the major clubs can be satisfactory even in difficult times.

4.   The German Bundesliga

The Bundesliga in Germany experienced a very interesting development over the past years. Although there was no major international victory of a German team since 2001 and the fact that the league is strongly dominated by only one club, the popularity of the Bundesliga has increased highly. In 2008 the German Bundesliga became the most profitable league in Europe with an "increasing profit of 168 million Euro (206%) to 250 million Euro".[15]In this analysis I will point out the reasons for the popularity of the Bundesliga and certain issues of German club football compared to the other three major European football leagues.

4.1   Strengths - The benefits of the 2006 World Cup

In 2006 Germany hosted the FIFA World Cup. One of the biggest sporting events was a big boost for German football. First, the attendance increased rapidly after the World Cup due to more interest in the sport. People from every social background attended the Bundesliga games which make the league the most profitable league in Europe with the highest average attendance.[16] Unlike the Italian league the facilities and the stadiums in Germany are so-called "supporters friendly". New stadiums all around the country make supporters enjoy attending the games which is financially highly beneficial (including the aspect of merchandising). Statistically, the average attendance from the season 2006/2007 to the season 2007/2008 went up by more than 400.000 spectators in the Bundesliga.[17] In

---

[15] Deloitte & Touche LLP (2008). *Annual Review of Football Finance*. Retrieved on October 17th from http://www.deloitte.com/dtt/article/0,1002,cid%253D56148,00.html
[16] Deloitte & Touche LLP (2008). *Annual Review of Football Finance*. Retrieved on October 17th from http://www.deloitte.com/dtt/article/0,1002,cid%253D56148,00.html
[17] See appendix (p 17) *Attendance table of German Bundesliga*

the season 2007/2008 Bayern Munich had an average attendance of 69.512 whereas Borussia Dortmund had an average of 71.650.[18] These numbers are evident for the popularity of the Bundesliga and the benefits of hosting the World Cup.

Germany hosted the World Cup very satisfactory which was recognized abroad as well. Therefore, European top class players traded to the Bundesliga. To my mind most of these players would not have moved to German clubs without the success of the World Cup. The modification of the stadiums and the financial boost for the clubs and the German Football Association make the Bundesliga a very interesting football league. Superstars like Brazilian Diego, Italian Luca Toni or Dutch Rafael van der Vaart traded to Germany and are examples for the international recognition of the Bundesliga.[19]

4.2 Weaknesses - The issue of competition in German club football

The quality of a sport league is dependent on competition. The more good teams play in a league the higher the interest and level of play. As mentioned, England and Italy have got four top teams. In Germany there is basically one club dominating the domestic league. Bayern Munich is the strongest team in the country and is financially much stronger than any other team. This lack of competition has disadvantages. First, Bayern Munich and its financial strength give the club the opportunity to buy the best players from other teams in Germany. This causes that the league not only suffers from competition within the Bundesliga but also that the second best or third best team will not be competitive in Europe on a consistent level. The fact that Chelsea is the richest club in England is advantageous for the club such as for Bayern Munich but teams like Liverpool or Manchester United are strong enough to compete. Top class teams in Germany such as Werder Bremen, Football Club Schalke or Hamburg are financially strong but there is a big gap between these clubs and Bayern Munich. The lack of competition within the Bundesliga on a top level (the average or weaker teams in the Bundesliga are financially closer) is one aspect of the failure of German clubs in European competitions.

---

[18] See appendix (p 17) *Attendance table of German Bundesliga*
[19] Explanatory note: Rafael van der Vaart traded from Hamburg to Real Madrid before the start of the season 2008/2009

4.3 Opportunities - Strategies of the German Football Association

From 1998 to 2002 the German national team was very unsuccessful and there were thoughts about how the German Football Association could improve the performance of the national team. By introducing a new system for the identification and development of talented German football players, the association emphasised on the national team rather than on club football. Especially hosting the World Cup 2006 was a major reason to focus on the national team. Unlike England, the German national team improved over years and reached the final of the Euro 2008 whereas the English national team were not able to qualify for the tournament. Therefore, German football is heading to an opposite direction than English football. Germany has a strong national team but problems to be competitive on a club level. England on the other hand focused on trading international players and improving club football. This caused that young English players had problems to improve their performance and strengthen the national team. This strategy of the German Football Association supports German football and its young players but on the European club level it means that teams from England, Italy or Spain are more competitive. Whereas Germany prioritizes the national team, other European countries focus on the clubs and its success.

Moreover, the German Football Association tries to restrict the possibilities of takeovers. It is seen as critical that foreign investors overtake German clubs including the fact that the positive outcome of takeovers on a long-term view is doubtful. Therefore, there is less money involved in the Bundesliga than in the English Premier League which means less investment in football players. It is simply impossible for German clubs to invest in human capital like Chelsea, Manchester United or AC Milan. Only Bayern Munich can be seen as financially competitive.

4.4 Threats – Financial disadvantages of German clubs

As mentioned the reputation of German football has improved intensively after the World Cup 2006 (see p 11). The fact that the attendance of the league went up over the years also means financial boost for the clubs and the Bundesliga. Even though, there is still a financial gap between the German league and the other three major league in Europe. The reason is that none of the German clubs have investors behind them who offer higher financial possibilities especially for player trading. In fact, there are better players trading to Germany nowadays but the difference between superstars from England, Italy or Spain and international players in Germany is significantly high. Except of Bayern Munich, which is a very wealthy club, other teams from Germany are financially weaker than other big clubs from Europe, especially from England. That means that higher investment of German clubs does not necessarily result in international success due to the financial strength of other clubs in Europe.

4.5   Future directions of German club football

To my mind the clubs in Germany have realized that they need to keep up with the major European teams in terms of investment and sporting success. Although the German national team and its development is highly important, clubs like Bayern Munich, Werder Bremen or Schalke will increase their investment in international top class players to be more competitive. The player transfers of the biggest clubs in Germany before the start of the season 2008/2009 show that the clubs adapted player transfer strategies from England or Italy. Germany has the advantage of having a solid national team and a high population which always offers new young domestic players to come up. I am firmly convinced that German clubs can find a good balance between German and international players to be competitive.

5.   Spanish football – Competitiveness of the Primera Division

Football in Spain has a huge meaning and it is based on high traditional values. In comparison to other major European football leagues, the Spanish Primera Division and its clubs have a huge traditional attitude. To be competitive and successful the clubs buy the best players from Europe and South America but the club officials stay away from overtakes or building new multi-functional arenas to keep their tradition. The two major clubs in Spain, Real Madrid and FC Barcelona, are one of the highest recognized clubs worldwide and both teams represent one of the biggest rivalries in world sport. In terms of quality, player trade and competitiveness the Spanish league can be seen as closer to the English Premier League than any other football league in the world. Besides Barcelona and Real Madrid, there are clubs who shaped up and perform very well internationally. Teams like Atletico Madrid, FC Villareal or FC Valencia are highly competitive in Europe and the fact that more Spanish clubs are able to get top-class players is an indicator for the strength and the good reputation of the league.

5.1   Weaknesses – Political divides of Spanish clubs

Unlike England, Germany or France football in Spain and its interest is extremely focused on club football. The national team of Spain has a much lower meaning than in other countries. The people are more proud of their club and their city rather than supporting the national team. This fact has traditional reasons. During the era of Franco in Spain in the 1930's a lot of different regions and people suffered from social disadvantages. Franco and his regime in Madrid murdered and tortured any opposition parties and its members, especially in areas such as Catalonia where Barcelona is located. Social disadvantages in areas outside of Madrid supported the thought of many people in Spain to be independent. Barcelona and Catalonia is one of the most extreme locations. Supporters of FC Barcelona despise Real Madrid and everything which comes from the capital. Especially after the reign of Franco, Barcelona fans aimed to have an own Catalan state and they are far away from feeling Spanish.[20] Catalonia is not the only one example in Spain. The basque region with its capital Bilbao is another area fighting for independency and there is a lot of resentment against the capital Madrid.

Unlike other rivalries such as Liverpool and Manchester in England or AS Roma and Lazio Roma in Italy where all the supporters are patriots, the rivalry in Spain is not only a sporting rivalry but politically backed. The history of Spain and its football clubs lead to the fact that a huge amount of people only support their local team. FC Barcelona, for instance, is a club with an impressive amount of supporters and fans even see this club as a religion. For the outcome of the national team the special situation in Spain has a huge impact. Whereas German, Italian, Dutch or English players are proud to play for their country, Spanish players other than from Madrid focus on playing for their local team. Players from FC Barcelona or Athletic Bilbao in particular have a different attitude towards playing for Spain. Due to the high meaning of Spanish club football the national team has never been successful over the past years.

---

[20] Marum, Jon (2008). *World Football: The Greatest Rivalries: Barcelona Versus Real Madrid.* Retrieved on October 17th from http://bleacherreport.com/articles/45906-world-football-the-greatest-rivalries-barcelona-versus-real-madrid

5.2   Opportunities – Reputation and tradition in Spain

The importance of Spanish football and the tradition attracts a lot of international players to play in Spain. Therefore, the quality of the Spanish league is increasingly high and much stronger than the Italian Serie A or the German Bundesliga.

Especially the squad of Real Madrid and FC Barcelona is extremely strong an equal to Chelsea FC or Manchester United although there is more money involved in the Premier League. International superstars such as the Dutch players Ruud van Nistelrooy, Arjen Robben or Rafael van der Vaart play for Real Madrid. Big talents such as Samuel Eto'o from Cameroon or Argentine Lionel Messi play for Barcelona.

5.3   Future directions of Spanish football

Due to the fact that the Spanish league has such a popularity and clubs have certain financial strengths I think the Primera Division will be one of the strongest football leagues in the world. There are no clubs in Europe with the tradition of Real Madrid or FC Barcelona which attracts a lot of world-class players to play in Spain. As for the national team I am of the opinion that it will be difficult to be equal to the domestic league. The importance and tradition of the Spanish clubs is simply higher than in other leagues which makes it unlikely that the national team will have the same meaning than in England or Germany. Even though, the unexpected victory of the Spanish national team at the Euro 2008 can lead into more popularity. It was the first title for Spain in football after 44 years but the constant success of Barcelona and Madrid on an international level is another indicator for the popularity of Spanish club football.[21] Therefore, there is no major threat for the Primera Division because the league is highly competitive and financially stable and the fact that the national team is shaping up is a positive aspect for Spanish football in general and does not harm the Primera Division.

---

[21] BBC News (2008). *Spain ecstatic at Euro 2008 win.* Retrieved on October 17th from
http://news.bbc.co.uk/1/hi/world/europe/7480521.stm

6.   Conclusion

In this paper I pointed out the significant differences between the major football leagues in Europe by focusing on the strengths, weaknesses, opportunities and threats. As mentioned in the introduction (see page 4) there are significant differences between the football leagues in England, Italy, Germany and Spain have led to a different status of each league in European football. English clubs, for instance are quite successful at the moment whereas German teams struggle in international competitions. To my mind the discrepancy has predominantly financial reasons. The more money involved the more good players enter the league and the higher the quality of play. England with its investors in the Premier League has huge financial advantages. No other football league in the world offers more investment in players and in the sport. Therefore, it is the best league in the world. Germany has a very profitable league due to the popularity after the World Cup. Even though, the quality of the Bundesliga is behind England and Spain. The Spanish league has a very good balance between high investment in players to be competitive but at the same time keeping the important tradition alive. Chelsea or Manchester United have lost their major tradition and gave it to international investors. On a long-term view it can be a concern to be overtaken by investors who do not care about local supporters or just see profits on a short-term basis. The Italian Serie A is the league with the biggest issues but is still highly competitive due to strong teams such as AC Milan, Juventus or Inter Milan. The SWOT analysis of each league not only revealed these differences it also shows that the future path of each league faces different challenges. If some countries and clubs handle these challenges better or face less threats, the competition within European football will lead into a higher discrepancy between rich clubs backed by investors and financial wealth and poorer clubs.

I am of the opinion that the level of the major European leagues should be more equal to assure the competitiveness of international tournaments and the interest of the supporters. A salary cap or a draft system like in the United States is a possibility but European football is another type of competition. In European football there is not only the competition of winning the league but also relegation or qualification places for international club tournaments (Champions League and UEFA-Cup). Therefore, the different leagues are divided into several different competitions whereas in American sports there is only the qualification for play-offs to win the league. Furthermore, a salary cap or a draft system would change the nature of the sport and it is difficult to implement in world football. I am firmly convinced that clubs who are financially too powerful harm the domestic leagues and smaller clubs suffer from it. At the moment the transfer fees and salaries are very high in European football and I think the major clubs will collapse at some point. There should be an ethical code between the richest clubs to prevent further increase in transfer fees and salaries. In the context of European football a mixture of the top four would be the best solution. The outcome would be the quality of play of the Premier League, the popularity of the Bundesliga, the tradition of Spanish football and the sporting efficiency of Italian clubs.

Appendix

I The 20 richest European football clubs[22]

Club (country)	Club value (in million £)
Real Madrid (Spain)	236.2
Manchester United (England)	212.1
FC Barcelona (Spain)	195.3
Chelsea (England)	190.5
Arsenal (England)	177.6
AC Milan (Italy)	153.0
Bayern Munich (Germany)	150.3
Liverpool (England)	133.9
Inter Milan (Italy)	131.3
AS Roma (Italy)	106.1
Tottenham Hotspur (England)	103.1
Juventus Torino (Italy)	97.7
Olympique Lyon (France)	94.6
Newcastle (England)	87.1
Hamburg (Germany)	81.0
FC Schalke (Germany)	76.9
Celtic FC (Scotland)	75.2
Valencia (Spain)	72.4
Olympique Marseille (France)	66.6
Werder Bremen (Germany)	65.5

[22] Cuddihy, Paul (2008). *Celtic are one of the world's top 20 clubs.* Retrieved on October 17th from http://www.celticfc.net/news/stories/news_140208090337.aspx

Club	Total attendance – Season 2007/2008	Average attendance (per game)	Use to capacity of stadium (in %)
Borussia Dortmund	1.218.054	71.650	88,25
Bayern Munich	1.181.709	69.512	99,44
FC Schalke	1.040.901	61.229	99,59
Hamburg	943.542	55.502	96,99
Stuttgart	865.874	50.934	91,32
Frankfurt	820.562	48.268	93,72
Nuremberg	743.258	43.721	93,46
Berlin	730.487	42.970	57,90
Werder Bremen	683.810	40.224	95,54
Hanover	669.808	39.400	80,96
Karlsruhe	495.511	29.148	86,85
Duisburg	417.613	24.565	78,26
Bochum	401.319	23.607	75,35
Wolfsburg	395.808	23.283	80,15
Leverkusen	360.753	21.221	96,99
Bielefeld	359.082	21.122	78,10
Rostock	333.413	19.613	68,10
Cottbus	264.891	15.582	68,50
Total attendance of entire season	**11.926.395**	**38.975**	**86,12**
Comparison Season 2006/2007	**11.518.923**	**37.644**	**83,15**

---

[23] Kicker Sport Magazine (2008, p 146). *Statistics – Season 2007/2008* (Published in German language). Nuremberg, Germany: Olympia-Verlag GmbH

References

BBC News (2008). *Spain ecstatic at Euro 2008 win*. Retrieved on October 17th from http://news.bbc.co.uk/1/hi/world/europe/7480521.stm

Becker, Gary S. (1994). *Human Capital*. The University of Chicago Press

Chadwick, Simon Dr. (2008). *FC Barcelona: Victory On And Off The Field*. Sport Marketing Europe

CNN (January 11th, 2008). *Man. Utd. Profits shoot up by 93%*. Retrieved on September 26th from http://www.cnn.com/2008/BUSINESS/01/11/manchester.united/index.html

Cuddihy, Paul (2008). *Celtic are one of the world's top 20 clubs*. Retrieved on October 17th from http://www.celticfc.net/news/stories/news_140208090337.aspx

Desbordes, Michael (2007). *Marketing & Football – An International Perspective*. Oxford: Butterworth-Heinemann

Deloitte & Touche LLP (2008). *Annual Review of Football Finance*. Retrieved on October 17th from http://www.deloitte.com/dtt/article/0,1002,cid%253D56148,00.html

Draper, Rob (2008). *Manchester City's billionaire wanted to buy into Arsenal*. Retrieved on October 17th from http://www.dailymail.co.uk/sport/football/article-1053144/Manchester-Citys-billionaire-owner-wanted-buy-Arsenal.html

FIFA (2008). *Yes in principle to 6+5 rule*. Retrieved on October 17th from http://www.fifa.com/aboutfifa/federation/bodies/media/newsid=684707.html

Harris, Nick (2008). *Chelsea climb into top five of world's richest*. Retrieved on October 13th from http://www.independent.co.uk/sport/football/news-and-comment/chelsea-climb-into-top-five-of-worlds-richest-781884.html

Jennings, Andrew (2006). *The Beautiful Bung: Corruption and the World Cup*. London: BBC 1 Documentary

Kicker Sport Magazine (2008). *Statistics – Season 2007/2008* (Published in German language). Nuremberg, Germany: Olympia-Verlag GmbH

Marum, Jon (2008). *World Football: The Greatest Rivalries: Barcelona Versus Real Madrid*. Retrieved on October 17th from http://bleacherreport.com/articles/45906-world-football-the-greatest-rivalries-barcelona-versus-real-madrid

Pfahler, Thomas (2000). *Human Capital and Efficiency* (Published in German language). Paul Haupt Verlag Germany

Shackleton, J.R. (2000). *Football as a business*. London: Westminster Business School